IMAGES
of America

QUANTICO

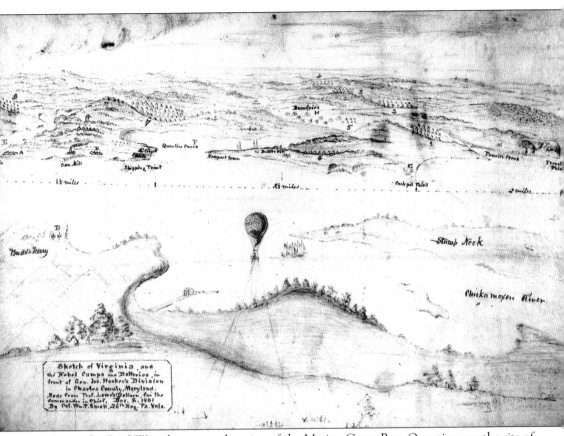

During the Civil War, the present location of the Marine Corps Base Quantico was the site of a blockade of the Potomac River by Confederate forces. Depicted here is a map of Confederate positions sketched from Professor Lowe's balloon. This is one of the first documented instances of aerial reconnaissance.

IMAGES
of America

QUANTICO

Mark Blumenthal

Copyright © 2003 by Mark Blumenthal
ISBN 978-0-7385-1502-1

Published by Arcadia Publishing
Charleston SC, Chicago IL, Portsmouth NH, San Francisco CA

Printed in the United States of America

Library of Congress Catalog Card Number: 2002116279

For all general information contact Arcadia Publishing at:
Telephone 843-853-2070
Fax 843-853-0044
E-mail sales@arcadiapublishing.com
For customer service and orders:
Toll-Free 1-888-313-2665

Visit us on the Internet at www.arcadiapublishing.com

BIRD'S EYE VIEW.   QUANTICO, VA.

Quantico, Virginia c. 1916 was a small town of limited purposes and home to the failing Quantico Company. A small pier on the Potomac River and access to the Richmond, Fredericksburg, and Potomac Railroad soon attracted Marines.

CONTENTS

ACKNOWLEDGMENTS

This book is dedicated to the Quantico Marines, including all those serving today, those who will serve in the future, and those who look back from these images. The pictures included in this photographic history are intended to reflect a broad range of the Marines and missions of Quantico over the past century, and are by no means intended to represent a definitive history. Recommended readings are provided for those who wish to conduct a closer examination of Quantico and Marine Corps history.

Of the many individuals who offered assistance in the preparation of this work, I would like to particularly thank the following individuals and institutions: Pat Mullen and Belinda Kelly of the Alfred M. Gray Research Center Archives; Lena Kaljot of the Marine Corps Historical Center; Fred Sullivan of Quantico Family Housing; Mitchel Raftelis, the Mayor of Quantico Town; and Ron Lunn of the Marine Corps Association. The images included here are official Department of Defense and United States Marine Corps photographs unless otherwise noted.

I would also like to thank the staff at Arcadia Publishing for the opportunity to share my interest in the history of Quantico. For her assistance in completing the initial proposal, I would like to thank Laura Daniels New. I am also indebted to editor Kelle Broome for her invaluable assistance in bringing this *Images of America* title to reality.

Culling the many photographs available for this project was a daunting task since the author has rarely found an old photograph without some interesting aspect. For her patience in helping narrow down the myriad of photographs in order to feature those serving the broadest interest, and for her many valuable suggestions concerning layout and caption content, I am most grateful to my wife, Anne Marie.

INTRODUCTION

In 1917, the United States Marine Corps was rapidly expanding in order to join the American Expeditionary Force that would shortly be heading for what would become World War I. To this point in history, the Marines had primarily been posted at U.S. Navy bases, fulfilling the Advanced Base Force role they had assumed after the Spanish-American War. However, Navy bases were becoming crowded, and were unsuited to prepare Marines to fight alongside the Army in Europe. Seeking to expand their military role, the Marines sought a training base with requisite maneuver areas and ranges. Having recently established new recruit training locations at Parris Island, South Carolina, and San Diego, California, Quantico was an ideal location for advanced infantry training of officers and enlisted Marines, as well as for a point of embarkation. Most Marines who served in the "War to End All Wars" completed their training at Quantico, and shortly after the close of the war the camp was purchased from the failing Quantico Company. As was the convention of the day, the post was named "Marine Barracks Quantico," stemming from the numerous Marine Barracks on United States Navy bases.

During the 1920s, the Marine Corps began a new era of expeditionary operations that protected American interests throughout Central and South America. Similar to those they had undertaken prior to the war, the Marine Corps undertook these missions as an extension of their role as "State Department troops," which protected America's commercial interests in this brief era of American colonial empire. Two decades worth of Marines sailed directly from Quantico aboard the USS *Henderson*, the first transport ship specifically designed to transport Marines, to Haiti, the Dominican Republic, and Nicaragua. Quantico also became a center of formal education when Major General Lejeune established vocational schools at Quantico. These schools later became the Marine Corps Institute. Formal military and vocational instruction conducted at Quantico eventually led to the renaming of Marine Barracks Quantico to the Marine Corps Schools in 1922.

During this period, Quantico and the Marines became synonymous in the minds of the American people through the skillful publicity efforts of senior Marines. One of those was the legendary Marine Gen. Smedley Darlington Butler, who led the Marines in a series of well-publicized Civil War reenactments using modern weapons, equipment, and tactics. These "summer maneuvers," demonstrating the capabilities of the modern Marine Corps on historic battlefields such as Bull Run, Antietam, the Wilderness, and Chancellorsville, drew enormous crowds. Butler also established Quantico as the home of the Quantico Marines football and baseball teams. Competing against college and semi-professional teams, they garnered an impressive 32-2-2 record, as well as nationwide publicity for the Marine Corps, in their first four seasons.

Visionary and innovative thinking characterized Quantico in the years leading up to World War II. Pete Ellis, a Marine Major, predicted the upcoming war with Japan and played a central role in developing plans to defeat the Japanese by capturing fortified islands in an island-hopping campaign, which was eerily prescient to actual events. Basing landing exercises primarily on Ellis's work, planners at Quantico set about developing the tactics, techniques, and procedures of the amphibious assault at Quantico and other locations. This culminated in the formation of the Fleet Marine Force in 1933. In concert with these innovations, formal schools for Marine officers at Quantico began tailoring the curriculum by including this new amphibious doctrine.

With the beginning of World War II came an exponential expansion of the Marine Corps. Ironically, the base where the revolutionary amphibious assault had developed was found to be insufficient for practicing the new techniques. New Marine bases on both coasts were acquired specifically to practice the large-scale ship-to-shore movements that were involved in an amphibious assault. Therefore, Quantico's focus continued to be research and development throughout the war and into the nuclear age, when Marine Corps training, education, and development was consolidated at the base.

During the Korean War, Quantico established several "Special Basic Schools" for Marine officers. At the end of the conflict, all basic and advanced officer training was firmly in place at Quantico. By the late 1960s, all research, development, and doctrine functions were also associated with the command. In order to more properly identify the current mission, Marine Corps Schools was redesignated as the Marine Corps Development and Education Command in 1968. In the mid-1980s, a new focus on warfare implemented by Commandant Gen. A.M. Gray, the base was again renamed the Marine Corps Combat Development Command in 1987. General Gray also directed the establishment of the Marine Corps University to bring the educational vision of General Lejeune to fruition. The University was established in 1989.

Today, Marine Corps Base Quantico is home to Marine Corps Combat Development Command, Marine Corps Training and Education Command, Marine Corps Recruiting Command, and Marine Corps Systems Command. Quantico continues to hold its title as the "Crossroads of the United States Marine Corps," due not only to the number of Marines who receive training here but to the broad influence the commands at Quantico have on the Marine Operating Forces, which are currently protecting America's interests worldwide.

One

WORLD WAR I
1917–1918

Due to highly successful recruiting efforts, the Marine Corps quickly found itself outgrowing training bases established at Mare Island, California and Parris Island, South Carolina. This necessitated the establishment of Quantico as an advanced infantry-training base for recent boot camp graduates.

An early view of Quantico shows Marines marching through town toward the Potomac River. The small town quickly adapted to the new arrivals with several cafés and a military shop. Tenting areas for the original bivouac site were along the banks of the Potomac.

Hotel Drusilla, Quantico Jct., Va.

Many newly arrived Marines frequented the Hotel Drusilla, one of the few available hotels in the area.

An early postcard shows some of the first buildings at the training camp. In the center is the Officer's Club. Clockwise, from the upper left, are the following: the Overseas Depot of the YMCA, the Knights of Columbus, the Gymnasium and Hostess House, and the Post YMCA.

Marines of the 136th Anti-Aircraft Company pose proudly next to their gun. As it became more apparent that aircraft would play a significant role in future conflicts, defensive anti-aircraft units such as this were formed.

11

Teufel Hunden

GERMAN NICKNAME FOR

U.S. Marines

DEVIL DOG RECRUITING STATION

NEW GIFFORD BUILDING

Pictured above and to the right is a rare visit from the Secretary of the Navy, the Honorable Josephus S. Daniels, who was instrumental in the acquisition of Quantico. The secretary is flanked on the left by Gen. John Archer Lejeune and on the right by Gen. George Barnett.

The Germans called the Marines "Teufel Hunden" or "Devil Dogs" due to their ferocity at the Battle of Belleau Wood. This recruiting poster quickly made use of the well-deserved nickname.

This postcard cover also makes use of the Devil Dog moniker. Quantico is still being referred to as a U.S. Marine Corps Training Camp, which points to its temporary status.

"Setting-up exercises" were conducted daily and usually were followed by calisthenics. These Marines are fortunate to conduct their exercises out of the mud due to constant improvements to the training camp, including wooden walkways and concrete exercise pad. Vigorous exercises and field marches kept Marines in shape prior to shipping out.

These young lieutenants undergo basic infantry officer training under the tutelage of a seasoned senior officer. The instructor is using a sand table in explaining tactical maneuvers to the attentive students. Interestingly, tables such as these are still used today, almost a century later.

This tenting ground was used to house visiting troops until barracks space became available. It was located on the site of the original hospital, in the area now occupied by the Communication Officers School.

This early postcard shows some of the buildings quickly erected at "Training Camp Quantico" by the Marines. The Quantico Bank building (center) served as the first headquarters.

15

Above is the 12th Regiment, Heavy Artillery on parade in the National Capitol during the winter of 1917. These Marines were some of the first to form at Quantico.

Christmas worship services in the newly completed chapel were particularly solemn as American involvement in the war loomed.

The ladies visible in the rear of the festively decorated chow hall wait for the arrival of the Marines and to begin serving Christmas dinner. Several recruiting posters are visible on the back wall.

This recruiting poster, by Howard Chandler Christie, was issued in 1915. An attractive woman modeling the Marine blue dress uniform was quite unusual for the day. The poster was very popular with the Marines, and other armed force branches used similar posters.

Reminiscent of Professor Lowe's observation balloon, which spied on Confederate positions at Quantico during the Civil War, these Marines ready their ZK-1 balloon for a practice flight in 1918.

The Marines of the balloon company trained at Quantico but were never sent overseas during the war. The unit was disbanded in 1921.

An early photograph of the Quantico training base was taken from an observation balloon. This is the earliest known aerial photograph of the Marine Training Camp.

Tractors such as this (which were essentially modified bulldozers) were used to haul guns through the thick mud found at Quantico. The springtime mud, which hampered Civil War soldiers 50 years earlier, earned Quantico the moniker "Slippery Mud Virginia."

The Heavy Artillery Battalion is shown in a staged formation with their three-inch artillery and the armored tractors used to tow them. Note the assortment of trucks to the rear and the

Heavy Artillery – Quantico – 1918

The first mobile artillery regiment poses in an artfully arranged formal photograph. Quantico Town is barely visible to the left of the picture.

unnofficial mascot in the front row.

A three-inch gun crew prepares to fire.

A three-inch field gun is towed to the gun park at the end of another hard training day. The Jeffery Quad truck is lost in its own dust cloud.

Jeffery Quad trucks were employed as the prime movers of three-inch artillery pieces. The "Quad" name comes from the vehicle's early four-wheel drive system. However, the Quad's hard rubber wheels had no treads and therefore the vehicle's mobility was hampered during Quantico's mud season.

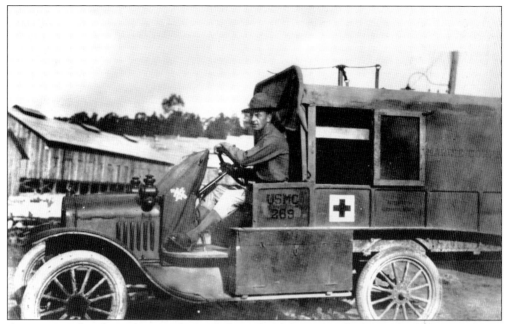

As was typical early in the war, this ambulance has been privately donated. The inscription to the right of the Red Cross symbol notes that Elizabeth L. Pearce presented ambulance no. 269 to the U.S. Marine Corps.

A machine gun school began at the Marine training camp. French instructors trained Marines to work the Lewis machine gun. Marines were tested on their ability to disassemble and reassemble the guns blindfolded.

As part of advanced training, Marine officers receive instruction on the nomenclature, functioning, and employment of many weapons, including these water-cooled machine guns.

A machine gun team, with rifles slung, prepares to move out. Their machine gun and ammunition is transported in an innovative cart.

The wide range of artillery equipment shown here in 1918 displays recent advancements in the science of artillery at the time. From left to right, the Marines use an artillery-spotting periscope, a range finding scope, and a plotting table. Those sitting in front of the artillery captain (the target recorder and field teletype operator) send fire missions to the artillery battery.

COMPANY STREET SCENE, MARINE'S TRAINING CAMP.   QUANTICO, VA.

A 1918 postcard depicts life at Camp Quantico. Note the ridge vent on the top of the barracks to let out the heat building up in the rafters during the hot Virginia summer, and the stovepipe for the coming winter. These Marines surely experienced Quantico's weather extremes.

These Marines are in a blur as they fall in for training in 1918. The confusion and highly polished boots signify that they are probably new arrivals.

The Post Exchange was always a favorite place for Marines. Although it appears the early exchange did not offer a wide selection, a particular beverage company certainly has gained an edge in providing refreshments. This view is from 1918.

This postcard shows a variety of activities at Miners and Sappers School, where portions of actual battlefields, such as Chateau Thierry, were faithfully recreated as part of the training.

Both officers and enlisted Marines share equally in the toils with mattocks and shovels as they dig zigzagging trenches in the Virginia clay.

Marines at the Miners and Sappers School, a forerunner of modern combat engineering instruction, dug the completed trenches shown here in 1918. Whole networks of trench systems were dug, the vestiges of which can be found in the wooded areas on base today.

Regiments were formed at Quantico and departed by battalions for France. Quantico sent approximately two battalions a month during the war, and this 1918 postcard shows one of the last battalions to depart.

Two

BETWEEN THE WARS
1919–1941

The permanent presence of the Marines called for a new administration building, erected in 1919, which served as the headquarters of the newly designated Marine Barracks Quantico.

The 15th Regiment, commanded by Col. James C. Breckinridge (seated to the right of the drum) departed Quantico in February 1919 for the Dominican Republic. Having formed

Now that the Marines will be remaining at Quantico, the muddy streets will soon be improved.

too late to participate in the World War, the Regiment instead served three years performing peacekeeping duties in Latin America.

This bridge covers one of the many low areas in the barracks area. The stream was called "the River Styx" and was later filled in.

The Quantico Hotel, which had previously been part of a resort operated by the Quantico Company, was acquired by the Marine Corps and became officer's quarters. This postcard is from 1919.

Two fire trucks and their crews protect the base from the ever-present danger of fire to the multitude of wooden barracks.

A view of the Quantico Shipyard shows the type of wooden ships built there for freight duty on Chesapeake Bay and the Potomac. The shipyard was the last remaining asset of the Quantico Company when it closed *c.* 1920.

The Quantico shipyard, shown here in full operation in 1919, operated on the same peninsula from which the Confederate batteries had harassed Union shipping on the Potomac River. The U.S. Navy Hospital was later built on the site.

"A Crusade for Right" was originally commissioned in honor of the U.S. Army's participation in the World War. However, the army refused to accept the statue as it accurately depicted a U.S. Marine, including a Marine Corps emblem on the helmet. Apparently, the artist unknowingly used a Marine convalescing in Paris as his model. Donations from Marines were used to purchase the statue and the local American Legion added plaques honoring the 5th Regiment, 6th Regiment, and 6th Machine Gun Battalion.

The administration building is shown here with the recently emplaced "A Crusade for Right" statue, 1920s. This statue is often referred to as "Iron Mike" due to its similarity to the actual "Iron Mike" statue located at Parris Island, South Carolina.

The Overton Hostess House welcomed generations of Marines to Quantico. The building's juxtaposed three-wing design makes it quite distinctive when seen in aerial photographs.

A group of recently arrived Marines take time for a group photograph outside one of the newer two-story frame barracks behind the Hostess House, 1920s.

Envisioning the stadium that would later bear his name, Gen. Smedley Butler initiated the construction of Butler Stadium and hoped to field a football team that would bring recognition to both Quantico and the Marines. The stadium was built entirely by Marines. The viewing stands were constructed using materials donated by the Richmond, Fredericksburg, and Potomac Railroad. Although the stadium is halfway completed here, the goal posts were in place and games were being played.

The Quantico Marines, shown here during a 1920 scrimmage, drew large crowds on game days. It was not unusual for members of Congress to travel to Quantico for weekend games.

Mr. Jiggs, the English bulldog purchased by Gen. Smedley Butler as a mascot for the Quantico Marines, was a most ardent fan. When a Navy bandmaster kicked Jiggs for refusing to yield the field during halftime, Butler ordered a charge of the opposing stands and honor was restored.

General Butler leads the cheer for the Quantico Marines at an away game in Philadelphia. The Post band and a large majority of Marines traveled by train to cheer on their team.

The 1926 Quantico Marines proudly display the President's Cup. The Marines were a highly competitive team, which excelled at all levels of competition as football evolved in America.

Though America's pastime was still in its infancy, the Quantico Marines baseball team was popular—especially with Mr. Jiggs, who felt that hot dogs were an important element of any game. During the 1920s and 1930s, most towns fielded teams, so the military team shared the baseball diamonds adjacent to Quantico Town that continue to be used today.

This early photograph depicts the Post Fire Department and the Marine firefighters. The station was near the railroad crossing into the Town of Quantico.

The Richmond, Fredericksburg, and Potomac Railroad (or RF&P) met the Alexandria and Washington Railroad via a bridge over Quantico Creek. Today, CSX, Amtrak, and the Virginia Railway Express (VRE) serve Quantico.

These artillery Marines conduct firing exercises on ranges at what is now considered the old combat area. The ammunition cart stands open to the left of the three-inch field artillery piece, and several expended rounds are visible.

Artillery Marines return from a day of training, 1920s. To Marines, catching a ride has always been preferable to walking.

Mr. Jiggs, in full flight equipment, takes a test hop to experience the thrill of early aviation during the 1920s. The pilot of the Vought VE–7 biplane is Gunnery Sgt. Benjamin Belcher, an enlisted aviator. The Marine Corps continued to have enlisted Marines serving as aviators into World War II.

The Marine Flying Field c. 1919 was quickly becoming the focal point of Marine aviation, as evidenced by the assortment of aircraft on the flightline adjacent to the new hangars.

Flights quite frequently ended like this nose-dived JN4 in the 1920s. Although injuries in this crash were minor, crashes in the early days of aviation cost many lives.

These Marines pose proudly in front an experimental pursuit plane in 1920. Seeking newer and better records in all facets of aviation, Quantico aviators participated in aerial contests and races.

Aviation legend Maj. Roy Geiger and his fellow Marine aviators flew four heavy bombers from San Diego to Quantico in 1920. This set several aerial duration records and saved the Marine Corps the expense of shipping the planes by rail.

The bombers acquired by the Marine Corps, such as this Martin MBT heavy bomber, were used in aerial bombing experiments. Note the unusual landing gear.

These ground support Marines pose outside one of the new corrugated steel hangars at the Marine Flying Field, 1920.

This seaplane is beached on the steep banks of the Potomac River. Later Seaplane hangars were built to accommodate the number of seaplanes acquired for use by the Marines.

HANGARS FOR SEA-PLANES.   QUANTICO, VA.

This 1920s photograph shows seaplane hangars for float planes and flying boats. The Marine Corps experimented with numerous designs for reconnaissance and anti-shipping bombing. Very few Marines stationed at Quantico today realize that the surviving seaplane hanger is now the auto hobby shop.

Secretary of the Navy Denby pays a visit to the Quantico aviators. Major General Lejeune, Marine Commandant, and Brigadier General Butler, Marine Barracks Quantico Commander, escorted the Secretary. Maj. Roy Geiger, Marine Flying Field Commander, conducted familiarization flights for the Secretary and Mrs. Denby.

This somewhat grainy aerial photograph is unique as it shows the 18th-century Dipple plantation in the foreground, which dates from at least 1724. The crash boat pier and Brown Field Number Two are also in view. The causeway, which parallels the RF&P tracks, connects the airfield with Mainside.

Minor crashes like this one involving a Vought VE-7 continued to be synonymous with early aviation. Fortunately, the pilot walked away only slightly injured in this case.

The Marine Flying Field was renamed Brown Field in honor of 1st Lt. Walter V. Brown, who was killed during a night exercise over the Potomac. Brown was a leading football player for the Quantico Marines.

Lieutenant Brown is pictured here with "Pooch" just days before his fatal crash.

The Marine Memorial Chapel was a non-denominational church serving the needs of the Marines and the civilian community. Today there are no churches in the town but residents are welcomed at services conducted at the base chapel. The building is now used as a Masonic Lodge.

A 1922 aerial view of Quantico Town looking east down Potomac Avenue toward the pier shows Marines marching through town. The large brick building in the middle of the photograph is the Marine Memorial Chapel.

Ordnance Marines test a field sling on a Lewis machine gun so that the gun may be employed during infantry patrols. Quantico's role in developing new equipment and techniques increased in correlation with involvement by the Marine Corps in "small wars" throughout the world.

Shown here is the "new" motor transport building, which displays a variety of vehicles used by the Marines. This building has been in continuous use and still serves as a repair facility for the base motor pool.

RESIDENCE OF COMMANDING GENERAL.   QUANTICO, VA.

The Commanding General's quarters were built on "Rising Hill" above the Quantico Hotel. This area was once part of the encampment site that supported the Civil War Evansport Batteries.

Built adjacent to the railroad depot, these distinctive twin buildings were constructed in 1919 and served as a receiving center and warehouse for the Marine Barracks.

Apartments such as these were the first permanent housing units for married Marines. Each three-story brick apartment building contained six apartments, which were referred to as "lettered" and "numbered" for officers and enlisted men, respectively.

These Marines are undergoing foreign language instruction using Edison wire recorders. The Marine in the foreground has casually placed his campaign cover over additional recorder spools. The distinctive campaign cover is still an authorized uniform item and has become the traditional headgear for Marine drill instructors at the recruit training depots.

While typing is not usually associated with the Marines, the vocational schools were intended to provide Marines with broad ranging skills. General Lejeune was inspired to turn Quantico into a "great university," and to that end established several vocational schools.

The famous World War I "Huns Kill Women and Children" recruiting poster by James Montgomery Flagg hangs in the foreground of the picture above. Flagg is most widely known for his "Uncle Sam Wants You" poster.

Marines of the Marine Corps Institute take time from their duties for a photograph. The Marine Corps Institute was an outgrowth of General Lejeune's vocational schools and was designed to allow Marines to continue their studies through correspondence. Today the Institute administers a variety of professional military education courses.

Even though the use of horses fell out of favor due to motorized transportation, Marine officers continued to receive equestrian training, such as in this "class of equitation," or as the Marines called it, the "horse course."

These Marines are participating in a daily study hall. General Lejeune established a training day consisting of military training in the morning and vocational studies or organized athletics in the afternoon. This emphasis on non-military training was controversial.

The Marine Corps established several trade schools at Quantico during the late 1920s to equip Marines with a trade for use upon reentering civilian life. Here wiremen string telephone lines through the town of Quantico near the RF&P railroad depot. The shack to the left was manned by railroad crossing guards.

This is a more candid study hall photograph. Both officers and enlisted Marines were required to study several hours each afternoon, although there seems to be little enthusiasm for study on this particular day.

Barnett Avenue is shown looking west. The post YMCA, a center for social and religious activities, and the post office are to the right.

BARNETT AVENUE AND FIRST STREET, MARINE BARRACKS   QUANTICO, VA

As roads improved and traffic increased the first control device, a manually operated "stop or go" sign, became necessary. This sign was manned during the training day at the recently paved intersection of Barnett Avenue and First Street, 1920.

A convoy of Jeffery Quads is seen returning from the ranges with three-inch guns in tow.

Several times during the 1920s, the Marines were called upon to protect the U.S. Mail from the threat of armed robbery. Marines headquartered at Quantico and San Diego guarded post offices, trains, and mail trucks. These Marines are armed with 12-gauge trench guns and .45 caliber pistols.

There were no robbery attempts while the Marines guarded the mail, which is not surprising considering these Marines are armed with .45 caliber pistols and backed up by a Browning automatic rifle.

Under the leadership of Brig. Gen. Smedley Butler, the Marines conducted numerous Civil War battle reenactments during summer maneuvers in the 1920s. Here Smedley Butler marches alongside a Private en route to a reenactment. Butler sought to publicize the capabilities of the Marine Corps by "re-fighting" famous battles with modern equipment and tactics.

Marines on the march trod the same Virginia roads and endure the same dust and heat as both Union and Confederate forces did 60 years earlier. Marines followed the original marching routes to reenactments as faithfully as possible. These roads appear little changed since used by Union and Confederate forces.

While most infantry forces marched to battle, trucks have replaced the "wagon trains" supplying the armies. Whether motor vehicles were more reliable was never satisfactorily resolved by these 1924 exercises.

A tractor quickly displaces an artillery piece during a reenactment at the Battle of the Wilderness in 1921.

Military police were indispensable for coordinating the movements of units and ensuring that the public remained safely removed from maneuvers and equipment at reenactments.

Any event involving the Civil War was certain to be a success in northern Virginia, and the country fair atmosphere added to the popularity of these events. Even President Harding, emulating President Lincoln, moved the operations of the White House to a canvas tent at Gettysburg to observe the demonstration. These events served to advertise the Marine Corps to many Washington politicians who were frequent guests.

All military evolutions consist of "hurry up and wait" phases. These Marines seem to be performing the former as they rush into positions.

Marines armed with bolt action, magazine-fed M-1903 Springfield rifles form a period shoulder-to-shoulder formation. The accuracy and volume of fire of the '03 Springfield would have exacted a terrible toll on a Civil War battlefield.

Rows of pitched "shelter-halves" in 1922 exemplifies the fact that encampments have changed very little since the Civil War, with the exception of the record player in the middle of the camp. Each Marine provides one half of the "shelter." Amazingly, shelter-halves are only now being replaced by modern tents and Gore-Tex bivvy sacks.

Peeling spuds on mess duty, shown here in 1921, may seem like a tedious task, but it is also an opportunity to socialize. More Marines also means the pile will be peeled quicker.

The chow line seems slightly top heavy with all the senior enlisted Marines at the head of it. Obviously, this predates the current tradition of Marines being served in reverse order of rank. Privates eat first! Note the various ways these "old salts" wear their campaign covers.

Marine Privates enjoy their chow. Most of the Marines have removed the Marine Corps Emblems from their campaign covers to avoid losing them. While the two-piece mess kits are found in surplus stores and antique malls, the venerable canteen cup is still heating up cocoa and coffee for Marines around the world.

A canvas-covered Post Exchange on the Manassas Battlefield offers Marines a few amenities such as three kinds of smokes, cold Coca-Colas, candy, and both pipe and chewing tobaccos.

Marines take a sandwich break on the historic National Battlefield Park at Gettysburg, Pennsylvania during a three-day reenactment in 1924, 61 years after the original battle.

Here ammunition is issued prior to a live-fire demonstration of the Marine Rifle Squad at the Antietam Battlefield near Harper's Ferry, Virginia in 1924.

Encamped here are Brig. Gen. Smedley Butler and his Brigade staff at the Wilderness Battlefield near Chancellorsville, Virginia in 1924. General Butler created quite a stir when he directed the exhumation of legendary Confederate Gen. Stonewall Jackson's arm. Lost as a result of wounds received at Chancellorsville in 1864, the arm was buried near the battlefield. However, General Jackson died days later and was buried in another location. The arm was reburied and a plaque was erected.

A balloon is readied for flight. Balloons were briefly fielded by the Marines as observation platforms. The baseball fields were used for these launches. Quantico Town is visible in the upper right of the photograph.

Balloon crewman may no longer be a military occupational specialty, but these 1924 Marines share much in common with present-day aviation Marines. Bandages on the Marine's hands in the center suggest the possible consequences of handling balloon tether lines improperly.

The USS *Henderson*, named after the 13th and longest serving Commandant of the Marine Corps, Col. Archibald Henderson, is shown docked at the pier in 1925. This ship was the first that was specifically designed to transport Marines.

The *Henderson* embarks the 5th Marines for service in Haiti in 1924. The *Henderson* served as a Marine troop transport vessel throughout the 1920s and 1930s.

The 5th Marine Regiment marches through the town of Quantico upon their return from Haiti in 1925. A train of the RF&P line crosses Potomac Avenue, and the Quantico Hotel, later to become the Quantico Officer's Club, is visible on Rising Hill in the upper left corner. The fact that Quantico was at one time the Marines' primary expeditionary base is not well known, even by today's Marines.

These Marines pose proudly in their "Blues." The "bursting bomb" over "crossed-rifles" identifies the Marine on the left as an Ordnance Sergeant. The Dress Blue uniform of this era does not have the distinctive red piping of today's Marines.

Lighters (barges towed by tugboats) were often used to move Marines and machinery. This lighter is a U.S. Navy car barge, and a large number of Marines are already on board.

This is a review of the 2nd Battalion of the 5th Marine Regiment conducted in 1927. Trooping the line from left to right are an unidentified adjutant (wearing campaign cover); Brigadier General Feland, Regimental Commander; Brigadier General Cole, Barracks Commander; and Major General Commandant Lejeune.

An interesting aerial of Quantico in 1926 illustrates the rapid growth of the post. The now-abandoned Quantico Shipyard is seen at upper right with the town just below it. The flagpole, in front of the barracks headquarters, is just visible to the left center, and the distinctive Overton Hostess House is visible at lower left.

The Harry Lee Hall Officer's Club is shown under construction. Named for Maj. Gen. Harry Lee, a three-time commander of Quantico, the club is now home to the Promotion Branch, Headquarters, U.S. Marine Corps. Engineers from 10th Marines quarried the stone locally.

Showing their age after years of continuous use, the "temporary" wooden barracks are soon to be replaced by "lettered" barracks. These distinctive three-story barracks will be constructed of brick and feature centralized heads and shower facilities on each deck, a galley and mess hall on the main deck, and open squad rooms.

Here is an aerial view of the barracks area under construction in 1926. The first three barracks are in staggered stages of construction. The gymnasium and Overton Hostess House are visible off to the left.

Excavation of the barracks' foundation was a labor-intensive endeavor due to the heavy clay soil typical of the area. Here laborers set drain tiles and place forms for the foundations to be poured next.

Roof framing on the first barracks nears completion in 1926.

The first two barracks are near completion and construction on a third begins, 1929.

The interior of a new chow hall located on the lower level of a barracks is shown here, 1930. The tables are set for the evening meal.

The base laundry handled a large volume of clothing and linens and was one of the largest employers of town residents and the wives of Marines.

An Honor Guard and Band lead a 1929 funeral procession for a Marine Private First Class through the town of Quantico to a small cemetery adjacent the base.

This is the 1929 Quantico Town home team, the Quantico Indians. Although this was the town team, Marine ringers were not uncommon. The town team shared fields adjacent to Quantico Town with Marine teams.

The Quantico Marines football team poses for a publicity shot in front of their bus and barracks, 1929. The success of Quantico teams was such that many towns and colleges vied for the prestige of having the Quantico Marines on their season schedule.

An interior view of a lecture hall in Breckinridge Hall in the 1930s is typical of the spartan interior of the school. The quotes hint at the new interest in amphibious operations forming in the naval services.

This is a picture of the Headquarters Marine Corps Schools, 1930s. The building is currently the home of the Marine Corps Command and Staff College.

Maj. Pete Ellis predicted a coming war with Japan and believed that the Marines would be the ideal force to conduct an island-hopping campaign against the country. Ellis also believed Marines needed the ability to conduct assaults from the sea. Ellis's prescience drove the Marine Corps to develop the amphibious assault. Ellis later died under mysterious circumstances while traveling on a "leave of absence" in the Japanese mandated islands.

In early landings, Marines would wade ashore from small boats. The limitations of small boats were clear even as the first exercises began.

An early amphibious exercise is conducted under a smoke screen near the Quantico Pier.

The dilapidated pilings give an indication that this landing is taking place near the former Quantico Shipyard area.

A group of foreign naval officers are photographed in the 1930s in front of an artillery piece affectionately named "Mae West." The gun crew is conducting a photo session of their own between the trails of the gun.

Demonstrations continue with the crew of a pack howitzer during the 1930s. Similar exhibitions for high-ranking visitors were common at Quantico due to the significant developments taking place there as well as the post's close proximity to Washington.

The Marines of the newly formed Fleet Marine Force demonstrate the capabilities of pack howitzers to a group of Marine Officers, most likely students of the "Junior Officers Course." The pack howitzer's size and weight made it ideal for amphibious operations.

An artillery battery is shown ready to commence firing, 1935. The gunners have lanyards in hand and gun crews face the rear with their heads down, awaiting the command to fire. It is doubtful they will receive the order, however, as the clearly staged photograph was taken at the main gun park and the barrels are pointing towards the barracks area and airfield.

An anti-aircraft machine gun crew is depicted in a posed photograph. These machine guns are cooled by water circulated through the "jackets" surrounding the gun barrels. A pump operated by the kneeling Marine provides cooling water to the gun.

Conditioning hikes are always part of an infantryman's life. The Marines in this 1930s photograph cross a makeshift bridge on the way back from the combat area ranges.

The howitzer section participates in a demonstration of Marines' capabilities.

Marines became world famous for their marksmanship during World War I, and later during international competitions. Shown here are Marines honing their skills on the rifle range at Quantico, 1920s.

This tractor, pictured in 1935, is able to tow a section of howitzers and ammunition carts.

The reason Marines were serious about their marksmanship can be discerned by the Record Practice sign. During the 1920s and 1930s, Marines became famous for their marksmanship acumen in worldwide shooting competitions. The basic Marine Corps tenet of "Every Marine is a Rifleman" was fostered in this era when Marines were paid a monthly stipend based upon their skills with the M-1903 Springfield rifle. Considering that a Marine Private earned $25 a month, the $5 paid monthly to an "expert rifleman" was a princely sum.

Quantico Town continued to provide for the Marines in the 1930s, and the Star Café was a favorite luncheon location. Mr. Raftelis, the proprietor who proudly stands in front of his business, took good care of his Marines. (Courtesy of Mitchel P. Raftelis.)

A mix of Marines and civilians hoist a few cold ones at the end of the day at the Star Café. The photograph is obviously after the 1933 repeal of prohibition, as indicated by the brand name beers available. (Courtesy Mitchel P. Raftelis)

The world famous aviator Charles A. Lindberg ("Lucky Lindy") and his aircraft make a visit to Brown Field in 1932.

The rapid expansion of Marine aviation quickly outpaced the capabilities of Brown Field; work was therefore begun on a new field encompassing the land between Mainside and Brown Field Number One. Extensive filling of the visible swampy area and construction of a channel to divert the Chompawamsic Creek are well underway in this 1931 photograph.

This Pitcairn Autogiro, designated XOP-1, was never officially adopted by the Marine Corps but was used during the 1930s in operations near Managua, Nicaragua (where locals referred to it as the "turkey hen") by Marine Squadron VJ-6M. The XOP-1 was the first rotary wing aircraft to be used in combat operations.

The planes of Aircraft One are parked at Brown Field in 1936. Visible is an assortment of aircraft, which includes the following: a Douglass R2D-1 cargo plane, the large aircraft parked near the rear hanger; a Ford RR-4 Tri-motor, which is shown taxiing to take-off position; and a larger number of Boeing and Vought fighters. The Marine Air-Ground Museum currently resides in the three large hangars. The runway has become the parade deck for Officer Candidates School.

The esprit de corps of the Marines is apparent among those who practice bayonet fighting with unsheathed 15-inch bayonets. This photograph was taken during the 1930s.

These 1930s machine gunners have revived the machine gun carts of their World War I predecessors. However, the guidon reveals that the Marines are part of the recently formed Fleet Marine Force (FMF). This designation replaced the former Advanced Base Force.

Marines disembark from a Landing Craft Infantry (Large), or LCI (L), on the banks of the Potomac in the 1930s.

A Landing Craft Tank (LCT) helps bring armor ashore in a 1930s landing exercise. The tank, an M-3A1 Stuart light with a 37-mm main gun, was to see service with the Marines in the Pacific.

General Breckinridge is shown here with his Marine Corps Schools Staff in 1933. The detailed arrangement of those photographed is interesting, the "attention to detail" inculcated among Marines, and evident in this photograph, was invaluable to the meticulous planning required for amphibious operations.

The "Reserve Area" is visible in the foreground of this 1937 aerial photograph. Other points of reference include the gymnasium, Overton Hostess House, barracks area, post headquarters, and 1919 building.

A dress parade at Marine Barracks Quantico was conducted in full Blue Dress uniform during the late 1930s. Originally a means of practicing forming for lines of battle, parades have become the standard means of commemorating changes of command, promotions, award presentations, and retirements. Sunset parades are similarly conducted at Marine Barracks 8th and I in Washington, D.C., and at the Marine Corps War Memorial in Arlington, Virginia for thousands of visitors each year.

The Marines, led by the post band, return to the barracks area after passing in review in 1937. The recently completed coal-fired steam plant provides steam for heating to Mainside.

The band strikes up a symmetrical formation in front of a lettered barracks in 1937.

The 1937 Quantico Marines team was photographed at Freeny Field. Completed in 1929, the field is named in honor of Lt. Col. Samuel W. Freeny, captain of the 1928 championship team. The bungalow-style homes in the background are on 5th Avenue in Quantico Town.

These Marines, who are recent graduates of the Basic School, will receive additional training at Quantico. The Dress Blue uniform is distinctive for the period. The officers all wear the "Sam Browne" belt, and the officer in the center wears a unique weapons qualification badge with suspension devices for each weapon with which he has qualified.

The Federal Bureau of Investigation Academy is shown here under construction in 1940. Seeking a training facility outside of Washington, D. C., the FBI established both a Training Academy and long-term association with the Marine Corps at Quantico. Today the FBI Academy and National Crime Laboratory occupy a highly secure 700-acre complex in a remote portion of the base.

Three

MODERN QUANTICO
1942–PRESENT

This is a ghostly image of Chopowamsic School as it appeared in early 1942. Government purchasing agents used the school to assess and purchase several hundred holdings, which would become range and maneuver areas for World War II expansion. Much of the area was vacant land, but there were numerous farms that had been in families for generations. Relocating caused some hardship due to limited housing in the area and higher property values driven up by wartime inflation. Today, Marines training in the Guadalcanal Area often discover the vestiges of former home sites including standing chimneys, old foundations, or even a fully standing house.

In total, Quantico acquired over 50,000 acres west of the mainside area in order to meet wartime expansion needs. This area was designated the "Guadalcanal Area" in admiration of the Marine Corps' recent successes in the Solomon Islands. These Marines, dressed in cold weather gear, march past one of the many small farms dispossessed to form the maneuver areas.

Snows at Quantico, though not unusual, are infrequent and usually light. Leading to the lettered apartments, John Quick Road gives an inkling of the steep hills that can turn even a snow dusting into an adventure.

The Calvin A. Lloyd rifle range complex is named in honor of Maj. Calvin A. Lloyd, who was the first Marine to win the President's Cup at the National Matches in Camp Perry, Ohio. The complex has three standard rifle ranges with 200-, 300-, and 500-yard lines for training and qualifying with standard service rifles. The range on the right has a 1,000-yard line for training scout snipers and conducting high-powered rifle competitions. To the right of the rifle range are four pistol ranges.

Maj. "Tony" Biddle, a champion boxer and unarmed combat expert, trained Marines during World War I and even into World War II, although he was by then in his 70s. Here Biddle conducts classes in fencing using a standard bayonet. He also taught bayonet techniques, which were based upon basic boxing skills.

Live radio broadcasts from military bases supporting war initiatives were quite common during the 1940s. The Blue Star Radio broadcast from the First National Bank of Quantico brought news about Marines in the Pacific and was a cooperative effort between broadcasters, the local community, and the Marines. The strong relationship among these groups of people was further strengthened during the war.

Shown here are station firefighters in front of their Buffalo fire truck. At this time the base had two fire stations, one on mainside and one on the airfield. Firefighters of the day were primarily Marines assigned to the fire department as a special duty. Due to the increased sophistication of suppression techniques and hazardous materials, fire protection today is provided by professional firefighters.

This is the U.S. Naval Hospital nearing completion in the 1940s at Shipping Point. This site was part of the Civil War batteries of Evansport, and was later home to the Potomac Ship Building Company. The remains of the shipyard are visible as a rectangular formation of pilings. Chopowamsik Island, the town of Quantico, and Turner Field (the recently completed Marine Corps Air Station named for Col. Thomas G. Turner, director of Marine Aviation from 1920 to 1929) are also in view.

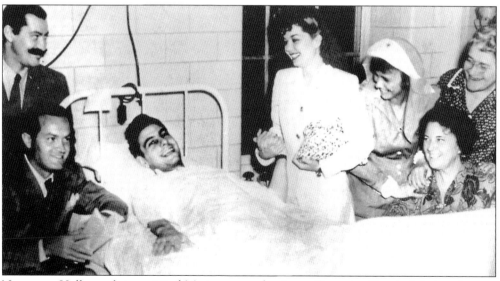

Numerous Hollywood stars visited Marines convalescing at Quantico Hospital during the war. From left to right are Jerry Colona, Bob Hope, Private Hughes, Francis Langford, Mrs. Mary Fenton, Mrs. Clarence Hughes (Private Hugh's mother), and "Mother" DeBoo. Mrs. Fenton, a Quantico "Grey Lady" volunteer, arranged this visit of the Bob Hope Show's cast members.

Waller Hall, the Commissioned Officers' Mess, is shown here around the end of World War II. Having served as an excursion hotel, officers' quarters, officers' club and mess, the venerable building stood another 20 years before succumbing to structural defects. During demolition it was discovered that it had been built directly over one of the Evansport batteries.

This picture is of the main gate at Potomac and Barnett Avenue as it looked in 1948. It is approximately three miles from U.S. Highway One. Upon entering the base proper, turning left and crossing the RF&P railroad tracks would bring one to Quantico Town; continuing straight would lead one to the Marine Base. Later, the main gate was moved to a position adjacent to the main highway.

This view is of Quantico Town in the late 1940s, looking east down Potomac Avenue towards the Potomac. The service-oriented aspects of the town have changed very little as many small restaurants, uniform shops, and barbershops continue to serve today's Marines.

"Iron Mike" serves as a backdrop for a group photograph of senior enlisted Marines in 1950. The administration building served as the base headquarters, and later as the offices of the Marine Corps Association, publishers of *Leatherneck Magazine* and the *Marine Corps Gazette*.

Pictured at the 1949 unveiling of a plaque commemorating the acquisition of Quantico are (from left to right) Gen. Clifton B. Cates, Commandant of the Marine Corps; Maj. Gen. Lemuel C. Shepard, Commandant Marine Corps Schools; and Mrs. Barnett. The plaque describes the cutting of a tree, symbolizing the acquisition of the Marine Training Camp, on May 5, 1917, by Franklin Delano Roosevelt (then the Assistant Secretary of the Navy) and Maj. Gen. Commandant George Barnett.

Training in interrogations was part of Marine Corps Intelligence School. Here a Staff Sergeant, with Korean War-era oversized collar chevrons on herringbone utilities, questions an aggressor force soldier. The enemy soldier obligingly points out the positions occupied by his forces.

Marines of the interior guard undergo "guard mount" inspection in 1949, and the unidentified mascot seems nonplussed that he is to be inspected next. Many Marines will recall checking in to the base here at the consolidated check-in center, the white building behind the formation.

Quantico was host to the Commander in Chief, President Harry S. Truman, on June 15, 1950. Truman was being influenced by many in Congress, who felt that the amphibious role of the Marine Corps was negated by the development of "atomic" weapons, and thus that the Marine Corps should be incorporated into the Army. The outbreak of war in Korea again demonstrated the Marine Corps' ability to rapidly expand, and convinced Truman that the Marine Corps' amphibious capabilities were essential.

This 1950 Korean War-era infantry officer training included an "attack by the numbers" amphibious assault. The Marine with the flamethrower is adding additional realism to the demonstration.

Marines had necessarily become experts at conducting assaults on fortified positions during World War II in the Pacific. Here officers are learning these techniques as they prepare to blast a bunker with a 3.5-inch rocket launcher, 1950.

Students of the Basic School in 1950 are given a demonstration of the capabilities of white phosphorous, or "willie pete," which is used for marking targets or incendiary action. As evidenced by this large class undergoing training prior to shipping off for Korea, Quantico's role as the central location for all Marine officer training was solidified during the Korean War, and all Marine officers since then have attended the Basic School here.

The outbreak of hostilities on the Korean peninsula caused a resurgence of the training of Marine officers at Quantico. Pictured around 1950, these Marines are viewing a 75-mm pack howitzer in a hasty firing position. The row of cedar trees behind them indicates the demonstration likely took place at an old home site.

Marine Officers are pictured undergoing instruction for tank and infantry coordination at the Basic School. The field across which they are moving was once part of a farm, as evidenced by the outbuilding in the foreground.

The Marine Aviation Technical School was established during World War II. In 1953, it became Larson's gymnasium and was named after Lt. Col. Emory E. "Swede" Larson, who was both a player and coach of the Quantico Marines football team. The seaplane hangars are visible near the crash boat pier, the building on the far right became the headquarters building for Officer Candidates School, and the aircraft to the upper right are parked on the present-day OCS parade deck.

Officer candidates of a platoon leaders course march past the OCS headquarters in the 1950s. The large metal hangar was once part of Brown Field Number Two and today houses Marine Air Ground Museum displays.

These officer candidates take a break from training for a visit to the Post Exchange. The Corporal behind the counter wears a distinctive, lightly-striped uniform. Women in the Marine Corps became fully integrated into the active forces, albeit in limited occupational specialties, after World War II. However, the uniforms were distinctly feminine and this trend would continue until the late-1960s, when uniforms were modeled after those of male Marines.

While it may seem this photograph was erroneously placed in the wrong decade, the "horse course" continued into the Korean War era. Horses and mules were pressed into service in the rugged terrain of Korea.

Wartime expansion brought the familiar site of Marines under canvas back to Quantico. Individual stoves provided heat to the tents on this cold winter morning. This tent area was maintained by Marine Corps Schools. The Marines are wearing helmets without camouflage covers, and the distinctive "herring bone" utilities, common during the Korean conflict.

These Marines are negotiating the obstacle course as part of basic officer training. Note that they do this with full equipment, which includes fixed bayonets on M-1 service rifles. The U.S. Marines were distinguished by their distinctive leggings. Today the Marines wear unique "digital" camouflage utilities.

This Marine helicopter pilot describes the usefulness and versatility of the helicopter to these newly commissioned officers in front of the Marine Corps Air Station in 1952. The helicopter was successfully employed by the Marine Corps in Korea on a wide variety of missions, which included observation, medical evacuation, and the first tactical lift of forces.

This aerial view shows a ceremony, most likely a graduation, held in Butler Stadium in 1952. Harry Lee Hall looks down from the woods at the top of Rising Hill, which commands an outstanding view of mainside and the Potomac River. John Quick Road, named for Sgt. Maj. John Quick, a recipient of the Medal of Honor, runs behind the stadium. The building in front of the Staff Non-Commissioned Officers' pool is the base brig, and the back of the base motor pool is visible at the lower right.

In 1952, Thomason Park Housing contained over 400 housing units for both officer and enlisted Marines, and was completed as a part of modernization projects.

108

Carl Gunnard Strandlund designed the Lustron Home, seen here. These mass-produced, all-steel homes have over 1,443 parts and an eye-catching porcelain finish in several pastel colors. With 66 in the Geiger Ridge and Argonne Hills housing areas, Quantico has the largest number of these historic homes in the United States. Established to produce economical homes for returning veterans and military bases, Lustron Corporation faced financial difficulties when production could not keep up with demand. The company went into receivership in 1950.

The apartment areas have been renovated to include enclosed sun porches on the ends of each apartment.

At the end of the Korean War, Quantico again focused on training Marine officers. Here Landing Vehicles Tracked, specifically LVT(4)s, of Marine Corps Schools conduct an amphibious landing on the shores of the Potomac. The need for such a craft was identified in exercises conducted at Quantico in the 1920s and 1930s.

These Basic School students, who are newly commissioned Second Lieutenants, operate a recoilless rifle during a winter training exercise in 1954.

Lieutenant General Cates inserts the first nickel into a Quantico Town parking meter in 1954. The meters were installed as a means to raise town revenues and have been a bane to many Marines since, yet improvements to the town have benefited all concerned. The gray building behind these gentlemen was the backdrop for the famous photograph of Generals Lejeune and Butler, taken 35 years earlier, on the cover.

Military police, armed with shotguns, escort the disbursing officer to the bank in Quantico Town in the 1950s. There has never been an attempt to rob the base payroll, likely due to the serious manner in which Marines undertake these escorts.

Completed in 1959, Liversedge Hall is named for Brig. Gen. Harry B. Liversedge. A confirmed bachelor and former Olympic shot putter, Liversedge commanded the 28th Marines, 5th Marine Division, during the Mount Suribachi flag raising on Iwo Jima.

This c. 1954 picture of the Marine Corps Air Station fire department shows an eclectic collection of vehicles. This station is actually located at Brown Field near OCS and is one of three fire stations, not including the crash crews on Turner Field.

A new guard shack was installed at the corner of Potomac and Barnett Avenues. A squared-away Marine is shown manning his post at the entrance to both the base and the town.

Shown here is the soon-to-be-completed Enlisted Club, Daly Hall, in 1957. It was named after two-time Medal of Honor winner, Sgt. Maj. Daniel "Dan" Daly. Little Hall (upper left), named in memory of Maj. Gen. Louis McCarty Little, a former Marine Corps Schools Commander, contains the Post Exchange, movie theater, and bowling alley. The base gas station and the entry gate (both visible, upper right) have since been relocated.

The base stables are visible in the foreground of this late-1950s photograph. Waller Hall is visible in the right corner above Little Hall. The hose tower on the backside of the building identifies the new base fire department.

New housing units were completed in 1957 above the lettered apartment area and became the "300 Block" housing area. These units were considered modern at the time due to their layout, storage areas, and off-street parking.

The headquarters of "Camp Hollister" (in reality known as Lejeune Hall) was featured in the late-1980s situation comedy "Major Dad." Many of the background scenes were filmed at Quantico during the four years the show aired. General Lejeune, who later became the 13th Commandant of the Marine Corps, twice commanded Marine Corps Schools. He was considered the "father of the amphibious assault," and Camp Lejeune in North Carolina, the world's largest amphibious base, also bears his name.

Shown here is Quarters One, the quarters of the Commanding General, after a late spring snow in 1958.

Camp Upshur, shown here in 1958 and named after Maj. Gen. William P. Upshur (a Medal of Honor recipient) was first established for platoon leaders classes in 1942, but served as home to the Basic School while construction was completed for its new home at Camp Barrett. The extensive use of Quonset huts and Higgins buildings was typical of World War II construction. Note the outdoor theater to the right of the water tower and the Blue Ridge Mountains on the horizon. Several reserve units make use of the camp today.

Here Second Lieutenants undergoing instruction at TBS make the move from Camp Upshur to the newly completed Camp Barrett in 1958.

116

These Lieutenants of the Basic School demonstrate the combined arms capability of the modern Marine Corps in 1955. Having marked a target by the fires of an M-48 tank, North American FJ-2 Fury commences a close air strike. Just as all Marines are trained as basic infantrymen, all Marine officers receive basic infantry officer training.

Here are the 1959 Marine Super Squad Champions. This competition pits Marine infantry squads against one another to determine the best. These Marines wear the new "sateen" utility uniform and flak jackets designed to protect the torso from shrapnel. The Marine Rifle Squad of today still consists of a Squadleader, Sergeant, and three fireteams of four Marines each commanded by a Corporal. Browning automatic rifles shown here have been replaced by the squad automatic weapon.

These odd-looking helicopters are YRON-1s. In this 1959 picture, they are being evaluated for use in aerial observation and courier duties by test pilots assigned to the Helicopter Development Squadron One, HMX-1. This squadron carried out many experiments to determine the ideal uses of helicopters.

The strangely shaped helicopters in this 1960s photograph are Piasecki HRP-1s, often jokingly referred to as "flying bananas." They were evaluated as potential troop carriers for ship-to-shore and tactical airborne movements. The dual rotor design is similar to that of the CH-46 Sea Knight currently in service with the Marines.

Here, a Sikorsky XHR2S-1 heavy lift helicopter is evaluated for use. The twin-engine helicopter, powered by two 2,000-horsepower engines allow it to carry 20 fully equipped Marines, was adopted by the Marine Corps in 1956.

This experimental hovercraft was tested extensively at Quantico as an alternative to landing craft for transporting Marines and equipment to the beach. Riding on a cushion of air, they proved to be successful modes of transport. Today the U.S. Navy operates large Landing Craft Air Cushioned (or LCACs) in support of the Marine Corps, capable of transporting heavy tanks or massive quantities of supplies ashore.

Completed in 1976, Lyman Park housing is the newest housing complex at Marine Corps Base Quantico. Virtually all housing areas are scheduled for demolition and replacement under a new program, in which a private contractor will build housing units and lease them to Marines and their families.

Quantico High School is unique in that all students are family members of active duty military personnel residing on Quantico. With the frequent relocating of military families, many students find themselves at Quantico High School for just one year while a parent attends a military school. QHS's close-knit environment creates lasting bonds, which bring back not only alumni but also those students who graduated elsewhere to homecoming.

By the 1970s, female Marines began to fill a wider variety of occupational specialties, including the military police. The MP shown here c. 1976 conducts traffic control at the corner of Potomac and Barnett Avenues during rush hour.

Military policemen here are posted in the Modified Blue Dress uniform, 1976.

The experimental nature of HMX-1s mission was transferred to the Patuxent River Naval Air Station in the mid-1960s, where Marine and Navy test pilots were involved in the design and testing of newer aircraft (such as the controversial Osprey). Shown here is an SH-3A Presidential helicopter landing on the south lawn of the White House. HMX-1 has the exclusive mission of providing helicopter transportation for the President. The "white hat" helicopters, including specially designed SH-60s, are maintained in a high-security area on board the Marine Corps Air Facility at Quantico.

The Marine Corps is unique in that the Officer Candidates School is conducted primarily by Staff Non-Commissioned Officers, who have a large role in selecting those who will become Commissioned Officers. The Marine Corps also commissions more officers from the enlisted ranks than any other service. Though it may not be readily apparent, these Marines are glad to have their platoon photograph taken, as it signifies that they will soon graduate.

The Officer Candidates School Headquarters building is seen from the "Grinder," on which candidates spend countless hours during the hot Virginia summer. One of the Marine Corps Air-Ground Museum buildings is on the right. The museum buildings will soon be replaced by the Marine Corps Heritage Center, near the entrance to the base and Interstate 95, which is expected to receive over 100,000 visitors each year.

The Leftwich statue is located in front of Heywood Hall at the Basic School. Lt. Col. William Groom Leftwich was killed in action in Vietnam and an award for outstanding Company Grade officers is presented in his name each year. Maj. Gen. Charles Heywood was the 8th Commandant of the Marine Corps. All Marine officers begin their commissioned service with attendance at TBS, where basic infantry officer skills are honed.

Marine Corps Combat Development Command Headquarters moved here from Lejeune Hall. The mission of the command continues to be the development and evolution of Marine Corps capabilities.

Shown here in 2000, the General Alfred M. Gray Research Center is named in honor of the 31st Commandant of the Marine Corps. Gray's focus on sharpening the Marine Corps's warfare abilities and emphasis on every Marine's Professional Military Education (PME) continue to contribute to the Corps's success. The statue "Molly Marine" is a tribute to women Marines.

The Marsh Building houses both the Manpower and Reserve Affairs and the Marine Corps Recruiting Command. It was named for Col. John Wesley Marsh, winner of the Silver Star in Korea and longtime civilian employee in the Manpower Division at Headquarters, Marine Corps.

This modern U.S. Naval clinic, photographed in 2000, replaced the old U.S. Naval hospital. The old hospital on Shipping Point has become home to the Marine Corps Systems Command, which is responsible for testing equipment suitable for use by the Marine Corps of the future.

The Marine Corps Exchange, pictured in 2000, offers a much wider range of merchandise and services than the PXs of the past. The MCX has a selection similar to that of most department stores or retail chains. The base commissary is visible to the left of the exchange.

The Marine Corps Association (MCA) publishes both the *Marine Corps Gazette* and *Leatherneck* professional magazines. The association also offers other services, such as insurance and printing, and operates bookstores at several Marine Corps bases, which carry many titles for the Commandant's Reading Program as well as a wide selection of military history books.

The FBI Academy is primarily responsible for training new Special Agents, but is also home to the FBI National Academy, which trains police officers from all over the United States and many foreign countries. The National Crime Laboratory and Behavior Sciences Unit are also in residence. The latter has been made famous in movies such as *The Silence of the Lambs*.

Located at the front entrance to Marine Corps Base Quantico is a scale replica of the Marine Corps War Memorial. The memorial depicts the flag raising at Iwo Jima, as captured by war correspondent Joe Rosenthal and published on the cover of *Life* magazine. "Iron Mike" and the Iwo Jima Memorial are the top locations for Marines and visitors to have their photograph taken.

SUGGESTED READING

Ballendorf, Dirk A. and Bartlett, Merrill, L. *Pete Ellis: An Amphibious Warfare Prophet 1880–1923*. Annapolis, Maryland: Naval Institute Press, 1997.

Fleming, Charles A. *The Crossroads of the Marine Corps*. Washington, D.C.: History and Museums Division, Headquarters, U.S. Marine Corps, 1974.

Johnson, Edward, C. *Marine Corps Aviation: The Early Years 1912–1940*. Washington, D.C.: History and Museums Division, Headquarters, U. S. Marine Corps, 1977.

Millet, Allan R. *Semper Fidelis: The History of the United States Marine Corps*. New York: Macmillan Publishing Company, 1980.

Poyer, Joe. *The M1903 Springfield Rifle and its Variations*. Tustin, California: Northcape Publications, 2001.